From the Inside Out

A Self-Esteem Book for Kids

Linda L. Lee and Jesse Lee

Illustrated by Tim Huesken

From the Inside Out: A Self-Esteem Book for Kids
www.lindalee.ca

Copyright 2005
1st Printing 2005   2nd Printing 2006
Published by 4th Floor Press, Inc.
www.4thfloorpress.com

ISBN: 0-9738179-3-3

Lee, Linda Louise, 1960-
From the inside out: a self-esteem book for kids / Linda L. Lee and Jesse Lee; Illustrated by Tim Huesken.
– 2nd ed.

1. Self-esteem – Juvenile literature. I. Lee, Jesse, 1994- II. Huesken, Tim III. Title.

BF723.S3L435 2006   j158.1'0834   C2006-903631-4

About this Book

Self-esteem is vital for all of us. The earlier we can learn about self-esteem and enhance healthy self-esteem the better. Self-esteem is what will provide the strength and resolve to be able to say "no" when you need to say "no" and to say "yes" when you want to say "yes". It is the armor that will help you emotionally survive bullying, being left out and embarrassing moments. Self-esteem includes self-confidence which enables you to try new activities and improve from mistakes.

From the Inside Out is geared for pre-teens and is designed to give information about what self-esteem is and how to improve it, if needed. The first part of the book includes text and some questions to discover your own responses to the information. The last part of the book allows for more detailed journaling and self-discovery.

From the Inside Out emphasizes the importance of self-talk and especially positive self-talk. It is easier to become aware of your inner voice if you can write out some of your thoughts. This book can be a valuable resource used by individuals or in group settings where discussion of the topics and examples are encouraged. The questions and exercises in the book can be used as points of discussion with parents, teachers, counselors, friends or other caring people in your life.

Acknowledgements

We continue to be deeply indebted to our family, friends and colleagues for their support and encouragement. This is the support that got us to launch and beyond. We are amazed by the willingness of countless others we have met on this journey who have helped take us to the present second edition - this includes bookstore owners and staff, authors, the media, teachers, physicians, counselors, organization executives and mental health professionals all interested and committed to the importance of self-esteem and children. We acknowledge the many parents and children we have met and conversed with regarding our books. We thank all of you for your valuable suggestions, guidance and inspiration for us to go further and farther.

What is Self-Esteem?

Self-esteem means liking yourself from the inside out. Self-esteem means liking who you are no matter where you are. Self-esteem means liking who you are no matter what clothes you are wearing or the size of those clothes. Self-esteem means liking yourself whether you are an honors student or have difficulties in school. Self-esteem means liking who you are whether you're in the popular group or not. Self-esteem means liking yourself whether you're a star athlete or not. When you have good self-esteem you like who you are and you have the confidence to show it. Self-esteem better equips you to stand up for yourself and what you believe in. It gives you the strength to be yourself and enjoy being who you are.

When you like yourself from the inside out, you believe you are a valuable person, worthy of respect, both from yourself and others.

Inner Voice

Sometimes it's hard to tell if you have good self-esteem. One way to start to discover your level of self-esteem is to notice your "inner voice." Are you aware of how you talk to yourself? Everyone has an inner voice-it gives expression to our inner thoughts. Your own inner voice can comment on things like your looks and your actions or the looks and actions of others. "Self-talk" is normal, but sometimes we are not aware of our own inner voice. And sometimes that inner voice can be quite negative. Negative self-talk can lead to lower self-esteem and vice versa. When you're unaware of your inner voice it can influence everything you do and say aloud. It can nag you, put you down and even make you feel horrible about yourself. You can change this negative influence by paying attention to your inner voice and what it's saying to you.

My Inner Voice

How do I talk to myself?

Take a couple of minutes, sit back and become aware of your inner voice.

Can you remember what your thoughts were when you woke up this morning? For example, did you say to yourself something like "Alright! Today we have gym... I love gym..." Or "Oh no, today we have a science test... I won't do well on it..."

My thoughts when I got up this morning:

____

____

____

____

My thoughts when I was going to ____________________:

(eg: school, lunch, home...)

____

____

____

____

Paying Attention to Your Inner Voice

Paying attention to your inner voice will help you discover if you tend to be either generous or mean to yourself. For example, if you don't do too well on a test, do you call yourself "stupid" or say to yourself, "I can't do anything right"? General statements like these can change the way you feel about yourself, and not in a good way. Instead you could say something more like, "Gee, maybe I need to study a little harder," or "Maybe I need to ask for some help."

Do you look in the mirror and say to yourself, "I'm ugly" or "I'm fat"? Or do you have a more positive focus with inner statements like, "I like my hair today" even if it isn't perfect, or kind of shrug it off by admitting that today could be "a bad hair day"?

If your friends are not paying attention to you, do you say to yourself, "Nobody likes me"? Or do you think, "Maybe they have something else on their mind," or "Maybe I need to hang out with somebody else"?

If you have a difficult game, do you call yourself "a loser," or do you tell yourself that things will go better next time?

Think of how good it feels when someone pays you a compliment, or when a friend says something to you to make you feel better. It feels just as good when your inner voice says positive things to you.

Paying Attention to My Inner Voice

Tougher Ones

Paying attention to your inner voice is an important step in discovering who you are. By asking yourself tougher questions, you get even more information about how your inner voice speaks to you. Answer these questions to find out if your inner voice is generous or mean.*

When I make a mistake what do I say to myself?

____

____

____

____

When I look in the mirror, what do I say to myself?

____

____

____

____

*See more questions in the journal section

Changing that Inner Voice

You'll notice that once you start paying attention to your inner voice, it will be easier to know if your self-talk is mainly positive or mainly negative. Once you become more aware of your inner talk, it becomes easier to change negative comments to positive ones, and it becomes easier the more you practice it. Every time you hear yourself saying something negative like "I'm ugly," or "I can't do anything," put up a stop sign in your mind and challenge the negative comment with a positive one. Say something like "I like this about myself," or "I am good at other things," or "If I practice I will get better."

When you become aware of any negative thoughts, try this:

STEP ONE:
Once you become **AWARE** of a negative thought

STEP TWO:
STOP IT

STEP THREE:
REPLACE it with a **POSITIVE** thought

OH CRUD...
MATH TEST
48%

I'LL NEVER ACE MATH...
NEVER!

WELL, I GUESS I DON'T STUDY MUCH.

POP QUIZ TODAY!

66%
WOW... WHAT A DIFFERENCE!

Inner Best Friend

If you are having trouble changing your inner voice to a positive one, it might help to create a "Shoulder Buddy." You can use your imagination to create your own inner best friend. You can always count on your Shoulder Buddy to cheer you on. Your inner buddy can help remind you to say positive things to yourself even if you are having a bad day. Your inside friend will remind you to be kind and caring to yourself as well as to others. This buddy on your shoulder doesn't talk back and doesn't give lectures. Your Shoulder Buddy will always find something positive to say to you. It will remind you about the things you can do well and about your good qualities. Your ever-present best friend can help remind you to like yourself from the inside out.

In addition to the importance of having a positive inner voice, liking yourself from the inside out also means things like knowing you are a good person, trying your best, knowing your likes and dislikes, trusting yourself, and having confidence.

Inner Best Friend

Draw a picture of your Shoulder Buddy saying something positive to you about you.

Do You Believe You Are a Good Person?

Do you care about others? Are you kind towards others and towards animals? Do you know the difference between right and wrong? Ask yourself these questions and listen to that inner voice. If you can say yes to these questions – great! If you have difficulty saying yes, perhaps your Shoulder Buddy can help you. Can you remember times when you know you cared about others or did something that you knew was the right thing to do? When that inner voice says something negative like "I'm not good enough," or "Nobody likes me," you can remind yourself of times when you knew you were a caring and kind person, or when you tried to do the right thing. These are qualities of a good person. Just like a good friend, a good person is someone people can count on and is respectful towards others. A good friend can give compliments to her friends without feeling she is less of a person because one of them is better at something than she is. You can probably think of other qualities that you would consider to be good qualities. For example, things you like about your friends or people who are close to you. Not only does it feel good to be a good friend to others, you want to be a good friend to yourself too. Be kind to yourself and care about yourself just as much as you do about others!

HEE HEE!
!

SARAH AND ANNIE WALK BY.
?

THEY MUST HAVE SEEN ME. WHY DIDN'T THEY STOP AND TALK TO ME?

SOMETHING MUST BE WRONG WITH ME.

MAYBE THEY DIDN'T IGNORE YOU ON PURPOSE. MAYBE THEY WEREN'T EVEN TALKING ABOUT YOU.

MAYBE I COULD GO SEE WHAT JENNY IS UP TO...

Do You Try Your Best?

One way to feel good about yourself is to try the best you can at whatever you are doing, or practicing to do better in activities that are difficult for you. Again, remind yourself about the times you successfully tried your best, even if the result wasn't necessarily successful. During those low times when things haven't gone as you had hoped, remind yourself with your inner voice (and good friend) about the effort you did put in to try your best. Making mistakes or having difficult experiences can be used as opportunities for learning more about yourself and others. And that learning might help you to make different choices or help you know more about what you like and don't like.

Trying Your Best

I tried hard when I ....

____

____

____

How did it turn out?

____

____

____

Was there anything I might do differently next time? (*Remember that it's okay to think about what you might do differently the next time. Making changes and making mistakes is part of experiencing things, growing, and learning)

____

____

____

Do You Know Your Likes and Dislikes?

Good self-esteem includes discovering what you like and dislike. Part of your identity is knowing what you like and dislike, and being able to tell others without feeling bad about it. This is part of what makes you different from others, and this is why your experiences will be different from those of others. So what you like and don't like may not be the same as what your friend likes or dislikes. You might like swimming and he might like skateboarding. You might like dancing, and she might like horseback riding. With good self-esteem, you do not feel that you have to make your friend like what you like, and you do not feel you must be wrong just because you don't like the same things as someone else. You might be getting advice or opinions (for example from TV ads) on what your choices should be, but more and more as you grow, you will be the one deciding for yourself what your own best choices are. You might change what you like and dislike over time too. Good self-esteem can help you to just have fun when trying new things, and it will help you not to worry that you won't be good at them, or that you might look silly in front of your friends. You have faith in yourself. You will know that you don't have to do something just to "fit in" with a group.

My Likes and Dislikes

Things I like:	Things I don't like:
Foods	Foods
___________	___________
___________	___________
Activities	Activities
___________	___________
___________	___________
School Subjects	School Subjects
___________	___________
___________	___________
Animals	Animals
___________	___________
___________	___________
Sports	Sports
___________	___________
___________	___________
TV Shows	TV Shows
___________	___________

Do You Trust Yourself?

Trusting in yourself means paying attention to your inner voice and to the feelings you get inside. If you get a gut feeling that something is wrong, you pay attention to that feeling. Your inner friend is trying to tell you something. Listen to it. Don't lie to yourself or ignore that feeling. Trust that inner voice and feeling and do what you think is best or what you know is right. If, for example, another kid tells you to try something that you know is wrong, and if he calls you a loser if you don't do it, you trust that feeling inside and listen when your inner voice says, "Don't do it." Don't feel forced to do something just because someone tells you to do it. A good friend will respect the choices you make. Having good self-esteem means taking good care of yourself, and this includes making good choices for yourself.

Trusting Myself

- When you get that gut feeling that something is wrong, pay attention to it!

- When you hear your inner voice or get that gut feeling, don't lie to yourself or ignore it

- When you know something is wrong take the opportunity to do the right thing.

- Trust your inner voice and feelings.

- Make good choices for yourself!

HEY KID!

GO UP ON THE ROOF AND GET OUR BALL FOR US...
DANGER! NO ENTRY

...AND WE'LL LET YOU PLAY FOOTBALL WITH US!
DANGER! NO ENTRY

THEY'RE JUST USING YOU. THEY MIGHT NOT EVEN LET YOU PLAY AT ALL!

NO THANKS.

Do You Have Confidence?

It is important to believe you can do things successfully.
This does not mean believing that you are better than everyone
else. It is a belief from inside about yourself. Pay attention to your
inner voice. Does it remind you of things you do well? Or does it
focus on things you have difficulties with? Your inner friend can
help with this too. Even if you feel embarrassed or nervous in a
situation, try to make sure your self-talk is positive and encouraging.
Think of your Shoulder Buddy cheering you on, reminding you
just to do your best.

Remember a time when you were learning something new. It might
have been difficult when you were first starting, and it probably
seemed like you would never improve, but as you practiced more
and worked at it, you did improve. Sometimes we forget about
these beginning times and how we overcame difficulties and
challenges in the past. When you believe in yourself, you have more
fun and feel even better about yourself. This creates a positive
circle of what you are thinking, feeling and doing. You think,
"I can do this," and you feel happier – and you might even improve!
Then think, "– I can do this even better than I thought."

My Confidence

What are my strengths?

What have I improved
with practice?

No One is Perfect

Remember that no matter how things seem on the surface, no one is perfect. Even that girl or boy you know with the perfect clothes or perfect hair or perfect body is just a person like everyone else. He or she will make mistakes too. The same goes with that girl or boy who seems to be good at every sport she or he tries, or with that boy and girl who seem to ace every subject without even seeming to try. Everyone will have struggles at times. Sometimes you will make mistakes. Sometimes you will wish you had done things differently or better. That's okay. If you like yourself from the inside out, you will not put yourself down. Instead you might think about what you can change.

Your inner voice can help you by asking you questions like, "What could I do differently next time?" Or "What do I need to do now?" Your inner friend can help remind you, "Maybe I'm not the best player on the team, but I still like to play the game." Or, "Maybe I'll play something different." Or, "I'll try to practice more." Remember even the best players make mistakes. Even kids who do well in one area, such as playing basketball, may have difficulties in other areas, such as in Language Arts class. Remind yourself of how you are unique and different in good ways. Your inner best friend can point out those times when you experienced feeling really good.

Be Your Own Best Friend

Remember to be your own best friend. Most people can be kind and caring to others. It is just as important to be kind and caring to yourself too. Self-esteem means taking good care of you. Taking good care of yourself does not mean you are being selfish. Taking good care of yourself means that you like yourself. You say nice things to yourself and you do nice things for yourself. You feel proud of the choices you make and the effort you put forth in activities. Your Shoulder Buddy can help you to be a good friend to yourself. Eating healthy foods and getting exercise are important, and taking care of our bodies from the inside out is important too! Take care of yourself inside and out.

DID I PRACTICE ENOUGH ?

WHAT IF THE ENTIRE AUDIENCE HEARS ME MAKE A MISTAKE ?

I HAVE TO THINK BACK TO THAT BOOK I READ! WHAT WAS IT ? SOMETHING ABOUT SELF ESTEEM...

IT SAID TO REMEMBER MY SHOULDER BUDDY ! IT SAID TO STAY POSITIVE!

DON"T FORGET HOW MUCH YOU PRACTICED. I'LL BE HERE CHEERING YOU ON THE WHOLE TIME!

60 MINUTES LATER...

HEY! I SAW THAT PLAY !! GREAT JOB !

AND TO THINK I WAS GONNA FRET OVER MY PERFORMANCE AND LET IT RUIN THE FUN WE HAD !

Getting to Know More About Yourself From the Inside Out

My Inner Voice

Additional notes on how I talk to myself

- Keep listening to your inner voice. The more you are aware of your self-talk, the more you get to know about yourself and your self-esteem.

Other examples:

My thoughts during class:

____

____

____

My thoughts while walking to the cafeteria:

____

____

____

My thoughts when I was with my friends today:

____

____

More on Awareness of my self-talk....

My thoughts before or during an after-school activity:

____

____

____

My thoughts when I was with my family:

____

____

____

My thoughts when I went to bed:

____

____

____

My own examples:

____

____

____

My Inner Voice-Tougher Ones

Tough situations can lead to negative self-talk. Think about these situations and what you might say to yourself in these types of situations.

Hint: Watch out for over-general statements such as "Nobody likes me" or "I can't do anything right".

When I have trouble with my friends, what do I say to myself?

____

____

____

When I am trying something for the first time, what do I say to myself?

____

____

____

Before a test, what do I say to myself?

____

____

____

When I don't do well in a sports activity, what do I say to myself?

____

____

____

When I think about an upcoming school activity such as a field trip or a school dance, what do I say to myself?

____

____

____

If I am meeting someone new, what do I say to myself?

____

____

____

Can you think of any other examples?

____

____

____

My Positive Thoughts

If you have become aware of some negative self-talk examples, it is important to challenge these negative thoughts with positive thoughts.

First write out some positive thoughts for yourself.

Hint: Look for things you like about yourself, what you do well, or what you could change. Remember, knowing that you can improve, asking for help, and making changes are very positive actions as well.

I am good at:

____

____

____

What do I like about myself?

____

____

____

What could I do differently?

____

____

Being a Good Person

Our positive qualities are not just about how well we perform at something. We can feel good about ourselves when we show care and kindness to others.

I showed I cared when I...

____

____

____

____

____

I was kind when I ...

____

____

____

____

____

Changing My Negative Thoughts

Now that you know some of your positive thoughts, remember them the next time you notice you are saying something negative to yourself.

Challenge those negative thoughts with your positive thoughts.

Hint: Remember to be kind and caring to yourself. Positive thoughts are like comments you would say to a friend who needs encouragement or cheering up.

Write out some of your own examples-this will make it easier for you to remember when you need to say these positive thoughts to yourself.

negative thought
STOP
positive thought
negative thought
STOP
positive thought

Remember when you filled out your likes and dislikes earlier in the book? Now, fill out a friend's likes and dislikes, so you can compare them to your own answers. It's okay to have different likes and dislikes from your friends.

My Friend's Likes and Dislikes

My Friend Likes:

Foods

____

____

Activities

____

____

School Subjects

____

____

Animals

____

____

Sports

____

____

My Friend Dislikes:

Foods

____

____

Activities

____

____

School Subjects

____

____

Animals

____

____

Sports

____

____

My Friend Likes:

TV Shows

____

____

Other

____

____

My Friend Dislikes:

TV Shows

____

____

Other

____

____

What do we like the same?

____

____

What do we both dislike?

____

____

What are our differences? For example, was there anything that you liked, but your friend didn't?

____

____

and that's okay...

Trusting Myself

Draw your own comic strip about a time when you trusted your inner voice. Fill each square with a picture of what happened:

The situation was:

I thought:

I felt:

I did:

How did it end?

Creating Confidence

Can you remember a time when you were starting something new?
Did it seem difficult and like you would never improve?
With practice and working at it, did you improve?

Describe this time:

____

____

____

What were you thinking and feeling at the time of starting something new?

____

____

____

What were you thinking and feeling after you improved?

____

____

____

Remember your strengths! You can improve!

My Positive Circle of Thoughts, Actions and Feelings

Write your own examples on the dotted lines

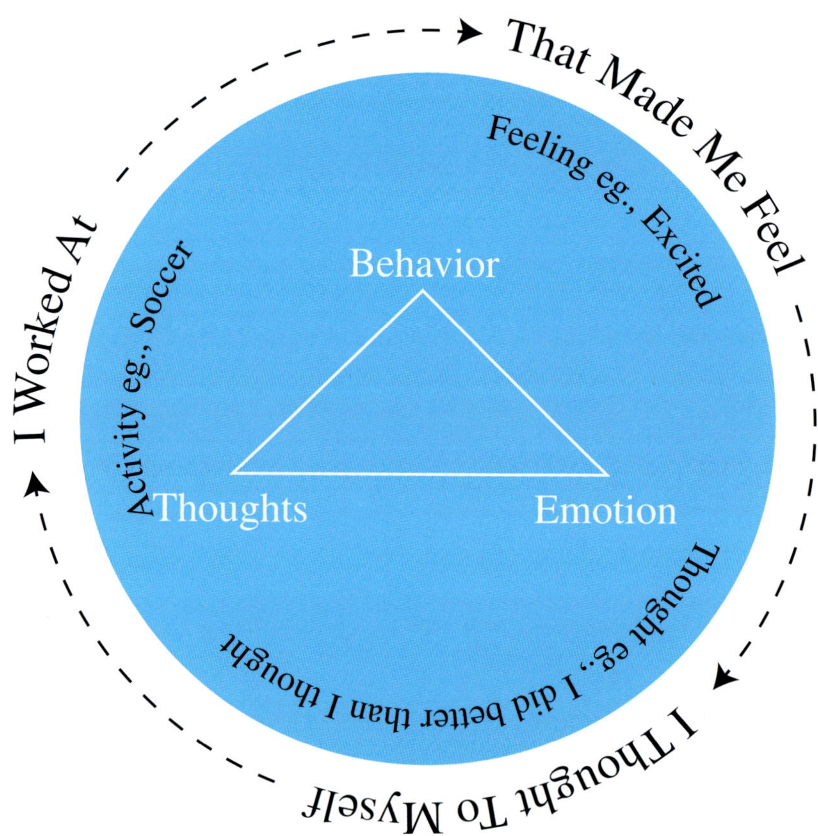

Being My Own Best Friend

Nice things I can say to myself ....

____

____

____

____

____

____

Nice things I can do for myself ...

____

____

____

____

____

Also available from Linda L. Lee and Jesse Lee:

Shoulder Buddies: Helping Kids with Self-Esteem (© 2005)

For Ordering Information or Comments and Suggestions, please visit **www.lindalee.ca**

About the authors – Linda and Jesse Lee

Linda is a psychologist in Calgary, Alberta. She specializes in the treatment of depression, anxiety and self-esteem issues for adults. Linda has co-facilitated self-esteem groups for over ten years. Jesse is a middle school student and specializes in homework. Linda and her son, Jesse, thought that sharing their discussions and ideas about self-esteem might be helpful for other kids. Jesse and Linda live with Kim (dad), Diego (dog), Zoe (cat), and Kozmo-the-pig (guinea variety).